20000885

P9-DDZ-271

ON LINE
ON LINE

JBIOG
Hamm
Torres, John

Mia Hamm

MIA HAMM

A Real-Life Reader Biography

John Torres

Mitchell Lane Publishers, Inc.

P.O. Box 200 • Childs, Maryland 21916

First Printing

Real-Life Reader Biographies

Library of Congress Cataloging-in-Publication Data
Torres, John Albert.
     Mia Hamm / John Torres.
        p. cm. — (A real-life reader biography)
     Includes index.
     Summary: Describes the personal life and soccer career of one of the top female soccer players in the world, Mia Hamm, who helped the United States win a gold medal in soccer in the 1996 Olympics.
     ISBN 1-883845-94-7 (lib. bdg.)
     1. Hamm, Mia, 1972- Juvenile literature. 2. Soccer players—United States Biography Juvenile literature. [1. Hamm, Mia, 1972- . 2. Soccer players. 3. Women Biography.] I. Title. II. Series.
GV942.7.H27T67 1999
796.334'092—dc21
[B]
                                                                          99-19949
                                                                         CIP

ABOUT THE AUTHOR: John A. Torres is a newspaper reporter for the Poughkeepsie Journal in New York. He has written fourteen sports biographies, including *Greg Maddux* (Lerner), *Hakeem Olajuwon* (Enslow), *Michelle Kwan* (Mitchell Lane) and *Darryl Strawberry* (Enslow). He lives in Fishkill, New York with his wife and two children. When not writing, John likes to spend his time fishing, coaching Little League baseball, and spending time with his family.

PHOTO CREDITS: cover:Al Bello/Allsport; p. 4 Pierre Ducharme/Archive Photos; p. 25 David Cannon/Allsport; p. 27 Stephen Dunn/Allsport; p. 30 Ezra Shaw/Allsport.
ACKNOWLEDGMENTS: The following story has been thoroughly researched, and to the best of our knowledge, represents a true story. Though we try to authorize every biography that we publish, for various reasons, this is not always possible. This story is neither authorized nor endorsed by Mia Hamm or any of her representatives.

Table of Contents

Chapter 1
What it Takes
to Win

When Mia Hamm was in college, her soccer coach Anson Dorrance spotted her doing something strange very early one morning. While almost everyone else was sleeping, he saw Mia doing wind sprints at a secluded park.

The coach was amazed. Mia was the best player on his team, and the most talented soccer player he had ever seen. And here she was, working out, before most people were even awake.

When Mia was in college she worked out all the time.

Coach Dorrance wrote Mia a letter telling her how much he admired that. She still has the letter. It says: "A champion is someone who is bending over to exhaustion when there is no one else watching."

With her dedication to hard work, it is no surprise that Mia has become the best female soccer player, and one of the best female athletes, ever.

Mariel Margaret Hamm was born on March 17, 1972, in Selma, Alabama. Mariel Margaret was the fourth of six children. Her mother, Stephanie, was once a dancer. She nicknamed her daughter Mia, after a ballerina that she had known. Her father, Bill Hamm, was a colonel in the U.S. Air Force.

Because of her father's military career, Mia's family moved around a lot. This was fun, because she was able to see a lot of the world. It was hard sometimes, too. Mia never got to really settle down. At one time or another, her family lived in Alabama, California, Texas, Virginia, and Italy.

When her father was stationed in Italy, nobody knew just how much it would change Mia's life forever. It was in Italy that her father fell in love with soccer. In Italy, soccer is as popular as baseball or basketball is in the United States. He loved watching it and he loved playing it. Mia was athletic and she loved sports. It wasn't long before she was playing soccer, also.

When Mia was five years old, her parents adopted an eight-year old boy named Garrett. Mia idolized her brother and followed him wherever he went. Soon, Garrett found that he loved soccer, too. He was a very good player.

Mia loved her big brother very much. It was very hard on her when

Because of her father's military career, Mia's family moved a lot.

Mia's brother Garrett was diagnosed with aplastic anemia, a rare blood disorder.

he was diagnosed with aplastic anemia, a rare blood disorder. Even though he had to take many medications, Garrett still played sports, and he was very good. He always looked out for his younger sister when they played together. "Nobody wanted Mia to be on their team because she was so little," said her mother, Stephanie. "But Garrett always made sure that he picked her."

When they played, little Mia would surprise everybody by how fast she ran. She was usually able to beat a lot of the older kids to the ball.

Chapter 2
Becoming an Athlete

Because Mia's family moved a lot when she was a young child, she did not develop a lot of self-confidence. It was hard leaving friends behind and it was even harder making new ones all the time. And when she did make friends, she could never be sure why they liked her.

"I always worried growing up that kids liked me because I was a good athlete," she admitted. "I did not have a lot of self-confidence."

Mia's entire family loved sports. In fact, her whole family played

Mia's entire family liked sports.

sports, and they supported her when she wanted to play. As Mia grew older, she enjoyed playing many different sports. She was very good at football and soccer. Being one of the youngest, and also being small, made Mia try even harder at sports, especially when Garrett was around.

"I always wanted to participate with my older brother because he was such a good athlete," she said. "I would do anything to play on his team."

Mia was always very competi–tive. She hated to lose.

Mia was always very competitive. She hated to lose. Sometimes, Mia would quit if she were losing. She thought that if she quit the game before it was over, then it didn't count as losing. Sometimes her brothers and sisters did not like that and would not let her play.

In 1982, a major soccer tournament, called the World Cup, was being played in Spain. The World

Cup tournament involves soccer teams from many countries. It is played every four years. Mia and her family watched almost every game. They had to watch the games on Spanish television stations, because those stations were the only ones that broadcast the World Cup games. After every game, Mia and her brother Garrett would run outside and play soccer.

When she was in middle school in Texas, Mia started to make a lot of friends while playing sports. She played Little League baseball and even made it on the all-boys football team at school. She played wide receiver and kicker. Mia didn't just make the team, she was one of the best players. But as she got older, the boys grew bigger. Mia realized that she was too small to keep playing football. She could get seriously hurt.

As Mia grew older, she realized she couldn't keep playing football with the boys. She could get hurt.

Mia soon realized that her future was soccer. It was, after all, her best sport. Mia dominated local youth soccer leagues and was even the best player on teams made up of the top players from different leagues.

When she got to high school, Mia decided to stop playing other sports and only play soccer.

Chapter 3
High School Soccer Star

When Mia started school at Notre Dame High School in Wichita Falls, Texas, she was an instant star on the soccer team. In 1985, when she was 13 years old, she was a Texas All-State selection in women's soccer—an amazing thing to happen to a girl so young.

That year, Mia was playing in a state all-star game when she was spotted by John Cossaboon, coach of the U.S. Olympic women's soccer developmental team. He loved what he saw. Mia was the fastest player on

In high school, Mia was an instant star on the soccer team.

the field. She outran everybody to the loose balls and she was able to see the whole field. Mia always knew what was going on around her. It was like she had eyes in the back of her head.

Cossaboon was shocked to learn that Mia was only 13 years old. After the game, he asked Mia to join the developmental team. The players on the developmental team were among the best in the United States. The team trained athletes for the U.S. Olympic Team. Cossaboon was saying that he thought she could become an Olympic athlete someday.

Mia started traveling around the country playing against the best players in the United States. It helped that she had moved a lot when she was growing up. Mia was already used to traveling, meeting new people, and making new friends.

After a year, Cossaboon called his friend, Anson Dorrance, to come

Mia started traveling around the country playing against the best players in the United States.

and see Mia play. Dorrance was regarded as the best women's soccer coach in the country. He was very busy, but he finally got to see Mia play in 1987.

"I'd never seen speed like that before in the woman's game," he said. "She had unlimited potential. She had incredible ability to shed defenders and get to the goal."

Dorrance asked Mia to play for the United States National Team. This was the next step up from the Olympic developmental team. Mia was only 15 years old, and she was playing against some of the best female soccer players in the world. "I loved how competitive it was," Mia said. "I was like, wow, look how hard these players work."

Later that year, Mia flew with the team to China, where they played against the Chinese National Team. Mia played well in the game. She did

Mia was asked to play for the United States National Team.

Mia set her sights on two things: playing soccer at the University of North Carolina, and, of course, the Olympics.

not score, but she did not allow the players she guarded to score, either. The United States won, 2-0.

By the time her junior year in high school rolled around, the Hamm family was on the move again. This time, her dad was stationed in Virginia. While it made Mia sad to leave her friends in Texas, she was happy to be moving closer to the national team's training site. She also liked her new school, Lake Braddock High School.

However, not everything was good for Mia and her family. Her brother Garrett's health was getting worse. His aplastic anemia was making his body weak. Garrett had to give up playing sports. However, he continued to encourage Mia, who had her sights set on two things: playing soccer for Dorrance at the University of North Carolina, and of course, the Olympics.

Chapter 4
Mia Goes to College

Coach Anson Dorrance had told Mia that he would give her a college scholarship when she finished high school. Mia couldn't wait. She asked Lake Braddock's principal about taking her junior and senior year classes at the same time. She was a very smart student and was able to do the work. It was a very hard year for Mia, but she proved that she could handle it.

Mia combined the two years and graduated in June 1988, a year early. A

Mia finished her junior and senior years in high school at the same time.

few days later she joined the U.S. team on a tour of Europe. It was good practice. In a few months she would be playing for Dorrance at the University of North Carolina.

When Mia started at North Carolina, the team was already great. The Tar Heels had not lost a game since 1985 and had won three college championships. Even though Mia was just a freshman, she played a valuable role. Mia was part of a powerful forward line, and she became a real scoring threat.

The team cruised through the regular season. In fact, they outscored opponents by more than 60 goals. At the end of the 1989 season, the Tar Heels won their fourth straight championship.

The next year, a lot of experts thought that the Tar Heels would not be as powerful as they had been. Their star player, Shannon Higgins,

When Mia started at North Carolina, the team was already great.

had graduated. Now, Mia would have to do most of the scoring. For a while, it looked like the experts might be right. North Carolina actually lost a game early in the season, and was on the verge of a scoreless tie with a weaker school. Then Mia took over. She scored the game-winning goal, on a little roller to the corner of the net, to send the Tar Heels on their next winning streak. When the 1990 season ended, the Tar Heels won their fifth straight college championship. Mia deserved a lot of the credit for continuing the North Carolina dynasty. She led all college players in scoring, tallying 24 goals and 19 assists.

When the 1990 season ended, Mia led all college players in scoring.

After her sophomore year in college, Mia had a tough decision to make. The women's World Cup tournament was being held in 1991, and a national team was being selected. Mia decided to leave college for a year to play with the World Cup team. She would be playing soccer, on a full-time basis, for an entire year.

One of the reasons that Mia decided to play was that soccer was not a popular sport in the United States. Women's soccer was even less popular. Few people would watch the World Cup tournament, unless an American team did very well. Mia and her teammates thought of themselves as pioneers. They wanted to show other Americans that women can play soccer as well as men.

Michelle Akers was the established star of the U.S. team, and Mia and Kristine Lilly were two of the younger stars. The American team was not expected to go far in the tournament. Mia and her teammates wanted to prove the experts wrong.

The U.S. team started strong. They beat Sweden, 3-2, then blasted Brazil, 5-0. After the Americans beat

Mia decided to leave college for a year to play on the World Cup Team.

Japan, 3-0, and then Taiwan, 7-0, the word was spreading: this team could play!

The U.S. team ravaged a powerful German team, 5-2, to advance to the world championship game against Norway. The game was close throughout and the score was tied at one goal apiece with just a few minutes left. Akers intercepted a pass and calmly put the ball in the net for the U.S. victory. The women jumped for joy. They swarmed each other and cried tears of happiness. Mia Hamm and her teammates were champions of the world.

In 1992, Mia returned to the University of North Carolina. She scored an incredible 32 goals and led the Tar Heels to another college championship. She was named the Most Valuable Player and the Player of the Year. The next year, Mia's final in college, she broke every college

In 1992, Mia returned to the University of North Carolina.

soccer record as the Tar Heels won the championship again. Mia didn't care about the records. She just loved being part of the team.

Coach Dorrance had tears in his eyes as Mia walked off the field for the last time in a Tar Heel uniform.

"There will never be a player who breaks Mia Hamm's records," he said through tears. "Never."

Chapter 5
Olympic Champion

Mia graduated from college in May 1994 and then on December 17, 1994, she married her boyfriend, Christian Corey. Soon after she was married, Mia moved to Florida to train with the national team. At the time, Christian was in basic training in the Marine Corps. When he completed basic training, he went on to flight school. Their individual commitments kept them apart for long periods of time.

Soon after Mia was married, she and the rest of the national team

Mia graduated from college in 1994, and soon after, she married Christian Corey.

headed to Sweden to defend their World Cup title.

But things did not go as smoothly there. China tied the U.S. in the first game. In the next game, against Denmark, Mia was forced to play goalie because one of her teammates was hurt. She admitted being scared to death, but helped her team out by making two key saves to preserve a victory. But in the semifinals, the U.S. team lost to Norway, 1-0, and had to settle for third place.

With the World Cup over, Mia and her teammates could now concentrate on the 1996 Olympics, which were being played in Atlanta, Georgia. The team was upset by its loss in the World Cup. They decided to start living together and training together in January 1996. They were determined to win the gold medal.

When the Olympics began in July, Mia was ready. She blasted two goals into the net as the U.S. beat Denmark in the first game, 3-0. In the next game, the United States defeated Sweden, 2-1, but Mia was hurt in a collision with a Swedish player. Her ankle was severely sprained.

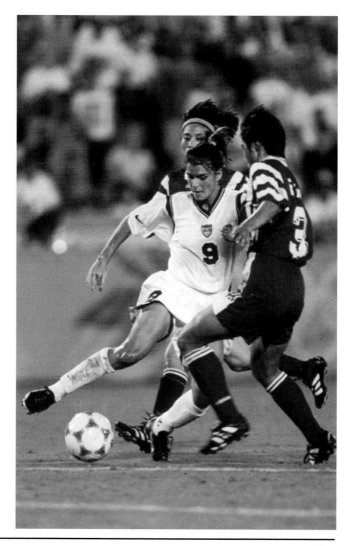

Mia, center, at the 1996 Olympic Games in Athens, Georgia.

Without Mia in the lineup for the next game, the U.S. team could not beat the Chinese, managing a scoreless tie. But the tie helped the United States make it into the semifinals.

In the next game, the U.S. team was scheduled to face its toughest competition, Norway. The winner would play for the gold medal. Mia wanted to play in the game. She taped her ankle and hobbled onto the field. She did not want to let her team down.

Despite her injured ankle, Mia played every minute of the game, even though she was knocked to the ground several times. Her tough play inspired her teammates. They defeated Norway in overtime, 2-1. The United States was now playing for an Olympic gold medal.

When the U.S. women's team took the field to face China for the gold medal, there were 76,481 screaming fans in the audience. They were chanting "U.S.A., U.S.A., U.S.A." for the entire game. It sent the hairs on the player's arms straight up. Mia could hardly walk, but there was

> **Despite an injured ankle, Mia played every minute of the game.**

no way she would sit out this game. The audience at Sanford Stadium in Athens, Georgia, was the largest crowd to ever watch a women's soccer game.

Mia did not score in the game but she was clearly the star. She hustled from start to finish. Nineteen minutes into the contest she blasted a shot that was deflected by China's goalie. Mia's teammate Shannon

Mia uses her speed to break away from a defender.

MacMillan tapped in the rebound for an easy goal.

Later in the game, with the score tied 1-1, Mia made an incredible pass to teammate Joy Fawcett, who raced down the sideline and passed to Tiffeny Milbrett. Milbrett slammed home the winning goal.

Mia was in so much pain that she had to come out for a substitution near the end of the game. As time ran out, the fans went wild. The team ran a victory lap around the stadium, waving to their cheering fans. Mia could not join them. She struggled to limp to the middle of the field and wave to the crowd.

"We all believed in each other and we believed in this day," Mia said. "We are an incredible group of people."

Mia's Olympic triumph was followed by personal tragedy. A few months after the U.S. team won the

A few months after the U.S. team won the gold medal, Garrett died.

gold medal, Mia's brother Garrett became very ill. After undergoing a bone marrow transplant he had developed an infection. His body was too weak to fight it off, and Garrett died in the spring of 1997.

"I have been blessed by so many things," Mia said. "But I would give back any of those victories to have Garrett's life back."

In 1998 and 1999, Mia was training for the next World Cup and was even thinking about playing in the next Olympic Games, in the year 2000. She had her best year yet in 1998, scoring 20 goals and 20 assists, and she became just the third player to score over 100 goals in international competition. As the 1999 season began, she was just eight goals away from the world record, 108.

She was named Female Athlete of the Year in 1998 by the U.S. Soccer Association. It was the fifth straight

Mia was named Female Athlete of the Year in 1998 by the U.S. Soccer Association.

year she had won that award. "Mia just got better in 1998," said Tony DiCicco, the coach of the national team. "She had the greatest year of any women's player in the history of the game."

Mia is constantly being interviewed and has been pictured on the covers of many magazines. *People* Magazine even called her one of the 50 most beautiful people in America. She has a contract to endorse Nike shoes and products, and that allows her to live a comfortable life with her husband.

Mia, always under control, splits the defense.

Mia, however, is never comfortable in front of the camera. She is only comfortable on the soccer field, a place she hopes to remain for a long time.

Chronology

1972   Mariel Margaret Hamm is born on March 17
1987   Becomes youngest player ever to joins the national team
1989   Attends University of North Carolina and wins her first championship in 1989
1991   Is the youngest member of the United States' World Cup championship team
1992   Set NCAA record for single-season assists (33) and points (97); coach Anson Dorrance calls her year "The greatest season ever by a collegiate soccer player"; named national Player of the Year
1993   named national Player of the Year
1994   named national Player of the Year; marries Christian Coey on December 17
1995   Led the U.S. national team in scoring with 19 goals and 18 assists in 21 games
1996   Helps U.S. team win Olympic gold medal
1997   Named one of *People*'s 50 Most Beautiful People In The World
1998   Scores 100th career goal; helps U.S. team win 1998 Goodwill Games.

Mia's Records

- All-time leading scorer in NCAA women's soccer history with 103 goals and 72 assists for a combined total of 278 points over 91 games.
- Led the nation in scoring in 1990, 1992 and 1993
- Scored more goals than any other player in Division 1 history
- Scored a goal once in every 4.1 shots during her college career with an average of 1.12 goals per game
- All-time leader in career assists with 72
- Registered 11 career three-goal games
- Set NCAA record for single-season assists with 33 in 1992
- Set NCAA record for single-season scoring with 97 points in 1992
- Holds NCAA Tournament career records for scoring (41 points), goals (16) and assists (9)
- Holds NCAA Tournament records for single-season scoring for points (16 in 1993), goals (6 in 1993) and assists (tied the record with 4 in 1993)

Index